Pageant of Seasons

A Collection of American Haiku

Pageant of Seasons

A Collection of American Haiku

by Helen Stiles Chenoweth

Illustrations by
JACQUELINE BLAKE

Charles E. Tuttle Company

RUTLAND · VERMONT: TOKYO · JAPAN

Representatives
FOR CONTINENTAL EUROPE
Boxerbooks, Inc., Zurich
FOR THE BRITISH ISLES
Prentice-Hall International, Inc., London
FOR AUSTRALASIA
Paul Flesch & Co., Pty. Ltd., Melbourne
FOR CANADA
M. G. Hurtig Ltd., Edmonton

Published by the Charles E. Tuttle Company, Inc.
of Rutland, Vermont & Tokyo, Japan with editorial
offices at Suido 1-chome 2-6, Bunkyo-ku, Tokyo

Library of Congress Catalog Card No. 78-134031
International Standard Book No. 0-8048 0546-6

First printing, 1970
Second printing, 1972

PRINTED IN JAPAN

To Harold G. Henderson

Table of Contents

Introduction

An interest in people and things Japanese has occupied three periods of my life that eventually led to the teaching of American haiku as part of work in creative writing classes.

When I was a child my mother read Japanese fairy tales and stories by Lafcadio Hearn to me. The story of *kusahibari* from his book *Kotto* was one of my precious memories of a "tiny insect whose particular kind of singing can be heard only in Japan." Years later I read his statement that poetry in Japan "is as universal as air. It is felt by everybody. It is read by everybody, composed by almost everybody, irrespective of class and condition."

This was a challenge to me when I first started to study the writing of poetry. One of the text books (now out of print) was used in experimental teaching of a second year high school class. First lessons were designed to write original poems in the haiku style and mood. In this experiment the

9

pupils became haiku conscious of counting syllables as well as trying to emulate the exquisite work of the Japanese poetry in American fashion.

The result was that a term later the first class of its kind in the eastern part of the United States was open to students of third year English and to others as an elective. The study of poetry beginning with haiku was the second part of my interest in people and things Japanese.

The third period came when I had a class in Adult Education, teaching a group of women in the Los Altos Writers Roundtable in 1956. This was a workshop among women who wanted to write poetry, prose, and articles for publication. Prosody, the study of poetic meter and versification, proved to have its stumbling block among some of the writers who could neither apply nor relate syllables to their poetic efforts. Recalling a book I had used and its discussion of the use of haiku with syllabic content, was a directive toward promoting the study of Japanese haiku. I used haiku alone to relate the understanding and use of syllables, followed by the cinquain for meter identification in writing. The form cinquain was conceived by the poet Adelaide Crapsey who promoted its use as an American form after she had made a study of Japanese haiku.

A dozen determined women formed a special class of dedicated haiku writers. The result was *Borrowed Water* (Tuttle, 1966). During this time I wrote many haiku as suggestions for class work and examples of American mood, idiom, season, and other themes for writing haiku. Most of these were preserved for *Pageant of Seasons*, all written in California where the actual pageantry of seasons is brilliant, ever-changing, and associated with scenes that are as unpredictable as snow on a full-blooming rosebush in February.

I wish to thank the editors of *American Haiku*, Platteville, Wis., *Haiku West*, Forest Hills, N.Y., and *Haiku Magazine*, Toronto, Can., for their permission to publish haiku which appeared in their publications.

Los Altos, California   H. S. C.

SPRING

Disciplined by rain
    white crane image distorted
      in dimpled waters...

Wind rage of March
breaks the hermetic seal
of sea's hibernation.

Lost in the blue haze
a solitary marsh hawk—
rising and falling . . .

Pampas grass
waving directions to speeding drivers
in wild March wind . . .

Spring's color swatches:
    black, tilled earth, barley green fields,
        golden winter wheat.

Eucalyptus trees
    in long lines of lashing rains—
        more trees and more rain.

Shine of swamp grasses,
    fringe of shimmering river—
        sun frames a picture . . .

Wind and the willow
   make their own patterns, defy
      the stream's roiled waters.

A blue jay was loved
   though he ate every berry
      prior to our picking.

Long line of white wash
   crayoned the air with clouds
      and one black shirt.

A wheeling bee
    ransacks flowering quince—
        drama of defeat!

Up high the freshet
    announces spring, then hurries
        toward the quiet sea . . .

Man's stomach hears noon
    in a whistle overhead
        and a young bird cries—

Importunate wind
  sends jays sunbeam-diving . . .
    man buttons his coat.

Soughing waters
  and vacancy sign on the house—
    the sea gulls cry . . .

In this strange garden
  the same notes, the same calls—
    birds of my childhood.

Archaic smell,
*   and yet spring's conscious green*
*   on moss-grown headstones!*

Boy snares the spring moon
*   in his water bucket and dreams*
*   of rocket ships . . .*

Spring rain pelting down
*   on winter's heap of dry leaves—*
*   sound disintegrates.*

Boy flying his kite
with authority in string
and his small hands.

That old rooftop
brags of spring in opera voice
of one mockingbird.

Gentle reminder:
for the first mockingbird's song
there is no title . . .

Liquid sounds of April:
   that bubbling in the orchard
      from one cow blackbird.

There is the quiet
   of crickets and tree frogs
      and one man thinking . . .

Those tossed peanuts
   fail to impress greedy squirrels
      with donor's blindness . . .

To shed a cloak
  of pain when seeing friends
    with spring's first lilacs . . .

That moonlight of spring—
  no soporific for crickets
    and mockingbirds.

Matching spring's wits
  the ball thrown by the boy
    chased madly by the dog.

Braided ivy vines
    held many bird songs but spring
        chose a single nest.

The grape hyacinths
    purple the garden path edge—
        no trespassing!

First, clowning jays,
    then saucy, thieving squirrels—
        and we have no almonds!

The stagestruck bird
   stood motionless in the grass—
    a shadow moved!

Popcorn flowers
   of catalpa on the spring lawn—
    children confused.

Spring tuning up:
   drum of grouse, whistle of quail,
    flute notes of robin . . .

A plate of cake crumbs
  persuaded old Town Crier jay—
    moment of silence . . .

Day in and out—
  even clouds do not distract
    yellowhammer's sun song.

Moonless the night
  that hides the dewdrops
    of the morning's sun . . .

Those happy raindrops
  splash tears and dismay
    on Easter silk dress . . .

Patches of clouds
  hatch boats on the still pond—
    insects ride free . . .

Reaching toward spring
  for all the Aprils to come—
    one white lilac!

In spring's overnight
   white violets lose shape, perfume,
    but not memories—

Canopy of trees
   waits stilly for the shower—
    man hoists umbrella . . .

Reading books about birds
   and their antics—a garden
    no longer lonely.

Deep organ music
    of a thousand bees persists
        in cherry tree bloom . . .

Spring's army aloft—
    waxwings on telephone wires,
        phone men wait below.

Neophyte architect—
    watching the bees working,
        a degree was earned.

Nesting sparrows
    madonna of her eyes on guard,
        no cat trouble!

Meadow-sweet lupin
    takes over with yellow hills
        like pigmy forests.

Flank move of towhee—
    linnet and sparrows scatter,
        a blue jay ponders.

Disciplined by rain
 white crane image distorted
  in dimpled waters . . .

That oblique shadow
 on the river bank, rolls down
  to a boy fishing . . .

A small frog sunning—
 to the depths of distraction
  a darning needle!

Past the shut gate of words—
child swinging slowly,
singing her own song—

Shining, crooked lane
bore no trace of pot of gold—
that deceitful snail!

In flooded rice fields
a wild mallard sits king-fashion
on a moon throne.

Bricks stack up
 through hot hell of off-bearing
  and a house is built.

Peace was premium
 with the bird's wild twittering—
  first fall from the nest!

Feather green branches
 lace a scowl of mountains:
  Corot is painting!

Possession: blue sky,
  rod, hook, and line,
    a small boy casting . . .

Date palm thrust three months,
  iris three weeks, yet the same growth
    of green daggers . . .

Crocheted by slow tide,
  those patterns of spindrift lace
    unraveled by waves . . .

That country walk—
  field flowers, spring bulbs in bloom,
    mezuzah on door's post . . .

Hazy quarter moon
  emptied its promise of rain
    on cactus paddles—

Mockingbird limit
  a telephone wire, but songs
    reach the heaven-fenced blue . . .

That heavy spring fog
  lowers to the tulip bed—
    our graceless table . . .

Mud-plastered posters
  of last summer's flower show,
    clean-washed in spring rain—

Graveyard platitudes:
  no meaning for spring's green moss,
    shine of melted snow—

Pecking and pulling
   at a bedraggled twig cache—
      two wrens promise spring . . .

Shorthand of dry weeds
   manages overnight change—
      row of crocus buds . . .

Fig tree's gnarled roots
   surfacing to make frames
      for white violets . . .

SUMMER

Bastion of evening sun—
a stray ray sentinels
the orange marigolds.

Wave-drenched, the rock
showed centuries of fossils
and one child bathing—

That dancing dancing—
petals of a white daisy,
a shredded letter—

"And where can you buy
that elusive perfume
of sun-dried laundry?"

Daily the pattern
   of many feet on ribbed sand
      the tide washes clean . . .

Of summer's saga,
   farmer with unhurried step
      gathers strawberries.

Breeze petaled the earth
   with catalpa popcorn balls—
      intolerant rake!

A foraging bee
centered in one full-blown rose—
emerged gilded . . .

Virginia bluebells
struck notes of summer's color—
singing picnickers.

Bastion of evening sun—
a stray ray sentinels
the orange marigolds.

Too sour for picking,
　the quail and their young eat grapes—
　　gloom of man and fox.

Those wild doves sit
　on the domestic clothes line—
　　babies quartered in field.

Shadow-fretted pane
　holds laughing image of child,
　　head crowned with roses . . .

Gust of shrilly wind
  beats pampas grass to the ground—
    an oak stands rod-straight!

Sound of weaving surf,
  a man whistling to his dog,
    plop of a small fish . . .

Walk a hot desert—
  see the Painter slash red
    across turquoise-feathered sky . . .

Those bamboo shadows
  melt into the garden wall
    sprayed with moonlight—

Shadowless noon
  removed time in purloined moment
    from sun dial.

Small tide finger
  obliterates evidence
    of sun-baked pebbles—

Man flattens out
redwood perpendicular
to sunlight and houses.

Clouds pursuing clouds
change quickly their many shapes
going nowhere—

The sun multiplies
light, shadows, and designs
on the racing tide—

Those seaward spaces,
  all Saturday-rented
    to many colored sails . . .

Boy's target a sun
  that splintered to a dozen
    as ball struck water.

Desert's total sun
  saps cactus shadows at high noon—
    small lizard confused.

A string of people,
  design of watching summer's tide
    aiming at cliff's top . . .

Receding drum beat
  of waves, then vacuum
    with one small bird cry—

Spring tangle
  of garden overgrown with weeds,
    irised with memories.

Calla lily
turns brown and shrivels
to cast out last week's rain—

Beauty and Beast—
wild honeysuckle tangle
covers charred cottage.

The incoming tide
gains majesty in caves
with Jovian thunder.

Searching adventure
  a child stares at an ant hill
    and finds a mountain.

A laughing boy
  splashed deep in the horse trough—
    a horse drank quietly.

Waves' glassy volute
  crashes into soapsuds—
    washes dirty sand floor . . .

In a carrot patch
   rabbits playing leap-frog,
      confusing kingdoms . . .

Those tree-building birds
   make their own way of life
      in forest of trees—

Fixed red butterflies:
   those poppies outlast the storm's
      early fall of nuts . . .

This country country—
morn does not waken from its drowse
till rooster crows . . .

Blue morning glories
outside the lathe house;
inside . . . blue morning glories!

That careful step
over cracked cement where mushrooms
show sovereignty—

There is certain peace:
frog on a lily pad,
lily in full bloom . . .

Reaching its goal
each incoming wave depends
on each incoming wave—

That duck's head bobbing—
but no water drunk
during courting ritual!

Cricket in a cage
  has no inspiration
    from summer's gay moods.

Earth-moving machines
  destroy vast orchards and summer;
    night remains star-filled—

For that first long mile
  man's journey was not wearing
    taken step by step—

Summer's long shadows—
the roadway does not relate
man to beast shape . . .

Mountain rim of fog
ballets to valley's quiet morn
with stealthy feet . . .

Cool, shady tree
offered giddy green umbrella
to hot noon sun—

That small garden cries
*   for want of accustomed care:*
*   gardener moonlighting—*

On the moon-tiled roof
*   a mockingbird plucked his song*
*   from the radio's voice.*

Border line of gold
*   speaks not of autumn days,*
*   but camphor trees declare!*

This old garden—
 hearing water meet water,
 smelling heliotrope . . .

Facing due west
 the scarecrow's shoe-button eyes
 each blaze a sun.

Grafting his body
 close to the autumn weeds,
 quail eludes hunter . . .

Scribble of weed:
  hanging to one withered leaf
    a pulse—beating!

Dancing like a gull
  over the smooth broad surges—
    a small fishnet ball . . .

Of black spaded earth
  the small golden suns—a patch
    of lemon cucumbers.

World lost in summer rain—
    lightning parts its curtains,
        the children are safe!

That man-in-the-moon
    stares face to face with the boy's
        water reflection.

Planted in cold shade
    of neighbor's fence, plumbago
        spills blue on my side.

Where once was bare sand,
freighted now with leaves and berries—
language of sun.

Magic! breathing salt air
of this Pacific—from whence
to where it goes . . .

In outgoing tide
small children race the low waves
like storm pelicans . . .

Time had closed its wings—
   fossils showed fish, insects, ferns,
      and millions of years . . .

Old pond world reflects:
   a cloud, a raft of grasses,
      one small frog chorus.

Showers of birds
   and long gone memories rose
      from old mission ruins—

Army of clouds
    driven to end of seeing
        leaves a naked blue sky—

Three slender birches
    hold the full moon in a net
        of their branches . . .

AUTUMN

By land and sea—
a small Japanese maple
sheds starfish on the walk...

Night's dark silences
enhance each note of cheer
in cricket's chirping . . .

Bobbing and rubbing
against rotting pier sides—
a spanking new boat . . .

So small an attic pane
to frame the vast area
of huge harvest moon—

Soporific waves
polka-dotted with many wings—
gulls dive for food.

Each swell of tide
carried autumn moon's bullion,
lost it to thieving sand—

One huge pompous wave
flattens out to a mirror
of surf board and boy—

Autumn comes with sounds:
one dry leaf slowly falling,
one nut plopping down—

This useless bread crust
thrown on the beach—but then
ten purposeful gulls!

Wings away from here
the siphoning of nectar—
pancakes with honey!

Yellow willow leaves
  drift in myriad patterns
    down the lazy stream—

Sometimes at dawn
  the wood's silence often screams
    with the first bird cry—

Blazing gold sunrise—
  abundant roadside weeds
    tipped with opulence . . .

Lace of spindrift
 on a well-pebbled beach—
  a mermaid's ball gown!

Is it the wind wailing
 or autumn's music when leaves
  are falling, falling?

The drone of flies—
 gentle persuasion against
  tree-cutting machines . . .

The flash flood roars
    over rocks, one bare point exposed
        and a moth rests—

Those grasshopper leaves
    lifted and laid down by the wind—
        lifted and laid down . . .

Shining brightly—
    that warm, soft harvest moon,
        as water receives it.

Dusty September—
  cotoneaster lights red
    in summer's late rain . . .

These golden flowers—
  a summer's glow to the garden
    in autumn's fog . . .

Recruited from beaches
  firewood burns with rainbows,
    fragrance, history . . .

By land and sea—
   a small Japanese maple
     sheds starfish on the walk . . .

Patching late garden—
   bare places bloom with color
     of old-fashioned quilt.

Sudden hailstorm
   left memories of thunder
     and water puddles.

Mirror of autumn sea
pictures setting sun
and one pale evening star—

Hunched mountains stood
sentineling the flaming sun
that displaced the sea . . .

Autumn's assurance:
acres of kaffir corn spears,
cattle food plenty.

Tiny jackasses
  penned behind sturdy fences—
    deer hunters fly free!

Squirrels on our rooftop
  with velocity of shot
    rolling their walnuts . . .

Blotting the vision
  of ocean horizon's freighter—
    those wheeling gulls.

Shining green volute
    breaks to sand, stones, spindrift lace,
    and surf-board rider—

Through the crashing noise
    of progress chopping down trees,
    a cricket's voice . . .

Scowl of rain clouds
    blackens serpentine rocks—
    a fortress rose . . .

A wave of asters
  purpled stark beach area
    with royalty.

A red sun ball drops
  outlining the smoke-blue hills—
    the night gains purple.

Gardener's choice:
  pinches back chrysanthemums,
    ignores the rose bush!

In late afternoon—
  a bastion of seagulls
    blotted out by haze.

That slick of oil
  drained off quickly in the stones
    carrying the moon.

Water registered
  the quarrel of clouds and moon
    with sudden blackout—

Those countless acorns
  if permitted to grow
    would people the earth . . .

Common weeds dried,
  sprayed with gold and silver—
    what uncommon weeds!

Beneath the huge rock
  tunnels, cellars, galleries
    of ants' history.

A spanking breeze
swished the decoy toward the weeds—
the ducks flew higher . . .

Small child picking weeds
understands the orchid gift
of his mother's smile!

Many small clouds will drink
from the spill of uptilted moon—
the rain comes . . .

That driftwood unpiled—
the shapes neither man nor beast
can recognize . . .

WINTER

By moonlight
    the silver-armored pines
    offer cold comfort—

Empty the wind
    with nothing but a meadow—
        white-flanneled with winter . . .

Hermit folk of dead weeds,
    reminder of summer's
        leafy multitude . . .

Carefully wrapped,
    sent special delivery—
        purple violets.

With their pink noses
the rabbits betray their presence
in the snow—

Winter's morning mist
walls the fishing boats—
a screaming gull breaks through.

A prize-winning garden
and pool, no evidence
of total planning years—

Viewing model home
    our vine-covered cottage
        became model home!

A child's first snowfall—
    laughter with realization:
        that nice rice pudding!

That scarecrow's coat
    bedizened with straw and snow
        and one corncob pipe!

The mountain was lost
in that first wondrous moment
the edelweiss bloomed!

Gift of white hyacinths
remembering a blizzard
and lost white poodle . . .

Homeless the sea's sound—
but sandpipers dancing
in the wind's howl!

Winter's still of air
  magnifies the man's approach
    to his silent prey—

Storm's effrontery
  laid tokens of leaves and snow
    at the open door . . .

This shining new bike
  and "visions of sugarplums"
    in small boy's laughter—

Winter crouched in fog—
somewhere a Swiss music box
played "good will to men."

Gull topples
in arc of magnificence
to discarded bread crust.

Fur-frosted tree
discarded, holiday finished,
kept Christmas for child—

These children come
   with largess of laughter
      and snow-filled hands.

They wait in silence—
   these many secret places
      the snow mountains hide.

By moonlight
   the silver-armored pines
      offer cold comfort—

Winter waves thunder
　high coastal crags, carry on
　　to whisper the inlet . . .

Flotsam and jetsam
　of tidal periphery
　　and no horizon . . .

That certain wind
　plays banjo music
　　in deodar's icy branches . . .

The wild geese fly south—
   man recalls former glory
    in perfect V-form.

A ribald stone fell
   out of harm's way; another
    caused a bad landslide.

With seaweeds unmoored:
   dark, surging cloud masses
    under water mirror . . .

Those shards of birds' eggs—
the issue of spring confused
by snow flurries.

Late setting of sun
paints fire-tipped points
on bristle-cone pine.

Weeds had established
their right to grow in Ming pots
that once held bonsai.

Searching winter's fog
  for intruders, lone starling
    posts on scarecrow's shoulder . . .

Winter wheat's greening
  in the grey uncertainty
    of spring's too soon . . .

Dry leaves whispering—
  wood fire defies lonely sound,
    crackles merrily.

That whilom chatter
　　of spring's birds often finds
　　　winter's logs burning.

Somebody lives there—
　　smoke from the chimney and smell
　　　of cabbage cooking.

So many birds at dawn:
　　the chatter and feeding
　　　and no mockingbird song!

The tiny "grass lark"
  fills the loneliness of night
    with opera music . . .

Wave obliterates
  sandpipers' hieroglyphics,
    rubber-soled shoe marks.

Pageant of seasons
  in snow's chilling presence
    on half-blown rose.

Thunder of rubble,
mad road work of giant tractors—
omnipotence!

A giant redwood
abreast the pigmy forest . . .
lopsided nature—

A sheet of paper,
an acre of trees and shrubs,
and one slim pencil . . .

Snow covers the field—
but the long line of blue stream
with early thaw . . .

Imprisoned yellowhammer
taps his window welcome
to spring.

Mountain peak's moment
erased by thunder heads'
black majesty.

Those cloud shadows
resting on scarecrow's shoulders
announce seasons change—

Annotated Bibliography

Basho, Matsuo: *Back Road to Far Towns* (Basho's *Oku no Hosomichi* with a translation and notes by Cid Corman and Kamaike Susumu). A Mushinsha Ltd. book, published by Grossman Publishers, and distributed in Japan by Charles E. Tuttle Co., Tokyo, 1968.

> The translators have not tried to present the Western ideas of haiku, but have admittedly preserved the Basho style which is terse and, because of unusual syntax, slow reading. This is a rich book that demands understanding.

————: *The Narrow Road to the Deep North and Other Travel Sketches* (a translation by Nobuyuki Yuasa of *Oku no Hosomichi*). Penguin Books, Baltimore, Md., 1966.

> This is a *haibun* (the prose equivalent of haiku) of such rare charm that it reads like a story. It is filled with haiku that are intrinsically part of the story, and not poetry so much as descriptions of Basho's travels.

Behn, Harry: *Cricket Songs*. Harcourt, Brace & World, New York, 1964.

>All the gentleness, the seasonal approach, the "reading-aloud" grace of haiku is in these translations.

Blyth, R. H.: *Haiku*. 4 vols. Hokuseido, Tokyo, 1952.

>Vol. 1, *Eastern Culture*, is a most searching compendium of haiku depths and origins, with material designed to please and teach the reader and writer of haiku in the English language. Vols. 2, *Spring*; 3, *Summer*, and 4, *Autumn and Winter*, contain the good haiku that Blyth found from "beginnings up to and including Shiki." Haiku by Basho, Buson, Issa, and Shiki are richly quoted and four chapters on their lives are necessary reading for the student of haiku.

Bownas, Geoffrey and Thwaite, Anthony: *The Penguin Book of Japanese Verse*. Penguin Books, Baltimore, Md., 1964.

>The haiku in this book were written in the Edo period (1603–1868); most of them by Basho, with a few examples by Buson, Issa,

and others. These translations are excellent studies of the works of Basho and several of his disciples.

Hearn, Lafcadio: *A Japanese Miscellany.* Charles E. Tuttle Co., Tokyo, 1954.

A group of stories, folklore, and studies, one section of which contains an absorbing and fascinating number of pages devoted to the history of dragonflies, with many drawings of more kinds of neuroptera than exist in any place in the United States. There is so varied a selection of haiku on the subject of dragon-flies that the chapter dealing with this insect should be part of any study of insects.

Henderson, Harold G.: *An Introduction to Haiku: An Anthology of Poems and Poets from Basho to Shiki.* Doubleday & Co., New York, 1958.

This edition is meticulously arranged with the author's English rhymed verse at the top, followed by the original Japanese verse and a literal translation. The selection is of necessity in numbers a sampling of the poets' most famous poems. Mr. Henderson carefully chose for translation sixty haiku which he believes "can stand alone in their present English translations." A book for every haiku writer.

———: *Haiku in English*. Rev. ed. Charles E. Tuttle Co., Tokyo, 1967.

This small volume has appropriate Japanese black-and-white sketches at the top of each page, enhancing the compact how-to-write-and-teach haiku.

Hoyt, Clement: *County Seat*. American Haiku Press, Platteville, Wis., 1966.

This book experiments with haiku and *senryu* (satirical verse), comprising variations on a theme by Chasei: "More, even than people / how many scarecrows there are / here where I live" (translated by Harold Henderson). The exemplary illustrations are by Vern Thompson. That so much could be written of interest about scarecrows in American haiku implies fascinating reading about the people who are found in any American setting of a county seat.

Kobayashi, Issa: *The Year of My Life* (a translation by Nobuyuki Yuasa of *Oraga Haru*). University of California Press, Berkeley and Los Angeles, 1960.

This book was written by Issa when he was a priest, and according to a postscript is "a thick and flourishing grove of poetry." It is a *haibun* containing both haiku and prose of a sort of enchanting travelogue. There is a fine variety of subjects in the many haiku.

Los Altos Writers Roundtable: *Borrowed Water: A Book of American Haiku*. Charles E. Tuttle Co., Tokyo, 1966.

The first anthology of original English-language haiku written by thirteen poets, members of the Los Altos Writers Roundtable, Los Altos, California.

Miyamori, Asataro: *An Anthology of Haiku, Ancient and Modern* (a revised edition of his *One Thousand Haiku, Ancient and Modern*, 1930). Maruzen Co., Tokyo, 1932. Reprinted by Taisedo Press, Tokyo, 1955.

Over 800 pages of haiku translations with annotations.

Nippon Gakujutsu Shinkokai: *Haikai and Haiku*. Tokyo, 1958.

The Japanese Classics Translation Committee in 1934 had for its objectives the translating of

Japanese classics into English to give West-
erners information on the cultural and spiritual
background of Japan. The Special Haiku Com-
mittee selected haiku for translation based on
intrinsic excellence, cultural and historical
value, and appeal to the Western reader.

Noyle, Ken: *Gone Tomorrow*. Charles E. Tuttle
Co., Tokyo, 1966.

A book related to the author's understanding
of Zen and poetry. There is no haiku study in
the poetry.

Rexroth, Kenneth: *One Hundred Poems from the
Japanese*. New Directions Books, James Laughlin,
New York, 1964.

A scholarly (bilingual Romaji and English)
book, fascinating and absorbing from the first
words of the Introduction: "It is common to
stress the many ways in which Japanese poetry
differs from English or Western European, or
for that matter, all other verse" to the last
lines of the Notes.

Southard, O.: *Marsh Grasses and Other Verses*.
American Haiku Press, Platteville, Wis., 1967.

The haiku in this book are of such excellence

that their reading enhances understanding of haiku in its American form. The contents, divided into four sections: salt-water, lowland, fresh-water, and highland, presents all the lure of the areas from which Mr. Southard derived his poetry.

Spiess, Robert: *The Heron's Legs*. American Haiku Press, Platteville, Wis., 1966.

The haiku in this book are varied in subject. Occasional rhymes make exciting patterns of reading the American form of haiku.

Stewart, Harold: *A Chime of Windbells: A Year of Japanese Haiku in English Verse*. Charles E. Tuttle Co., Tokyo, 1969.

About 360 haiku, with the same delicate, fragile beauty in translation as the originals written centuries ago. They are divided into the traditional four seasons, with a short section on the New Year. The thirty-three haiku paintings help to create the mood and atmosphere of the seasons. An essay by Mr. Stewart discusses the spiritual and religious tradition of haiku.

————: *A Net of Fireflies: Japanese Haiku and*

Haiku Paintings. Charles E. Tuttle Co., Tokyo, 1960.

> More than 300 haiku translated into the author's version of two-lined, rhymed haiku. Profusely illustrated.

Waley, Arthur: *Japanese Poetry: The "Uta."* Lund, Humphries & Co., London, 1959.

> This is an excellent book for the student who is interested in all forms of Japanese poetry. The *uta* is the verse par excellence of thirty-one syllables of which Mr. Waley says: "It might have been expected that the Japanese, having confined themselves for centuries to the five-line *uta*, would . . . have embarked on wider seas." The five lines were eventually contracted to the haiku of seventeen syllables and three lines.

Yasuda, Kenneth: *The Japanese Haiku: Its Essential Nature, History, and Possibilities in English, with Selected Examples.* Charles E. Tuttle Co., Tokyo, 1957.

> The well-arranged analysis and examples of Japan's outstanding literary form and its comprehensive history make this essential reading for English haiku poets.